POWER POSITIVITY

I AM GRATEFUL

Hardie Grant

BOOKS

IF YOU WANT TO CHANGE YOUR STATE OF BEING, START TO BE GRATEFUL.

Oprah Winfrey

GRATITUDE MAKES BAD DAYS BEARABLE AND ORDINARY DAYS BEAUTIFUL.

I'M GRATEFUL FOR LIFE ITSELF AND THAT I GET TO LIVE IN MY TRUTH AND THRIVE.

Laverne Cox

I'M THANKFUL FOR MY
MOTHER FOR BRINGING
ME INTO THIS WORLD.
I'M THANKFUL FOR LIFE.

Naomi Campbell

THE REAL WORLD IS HARD AND
YET YOU CAN STILL WAKE UP
EVERY SINGLE MORNING AND GO,
"I HAVE THREE AMAZING KIDS
AND I HAVE CREATED WORK I AM
PROUD OF, AND I ABSOLUTELY
LOVE MY LIFE AND I WOULD NOT
TRADE IT FOR ANYONE ELSE'S
LIFE EVER."

Shonda Rhimes

THE BEST VIEW COMES AFTER THE HARDEST CLIMB.

WE SHOULD ALL TAKE ONE
MORE MOMENT TO THANK OUR
LOVED ONES FOR BEING HERE
AND FOR BEING A SOURCE
OF LOVE AND SUPPORT
THROUGHOUT THE JOURNEY
THAT LED US TO THIS MOMENT.

Kerry Washington

WOMEN ARE LEARNING THAT WE CAN BE GRATEFUL FOR WHAT WE HAVE AND ALSO DEMAND WHAT WE DESERVE.

Abby Wambach

I THINK I'VE JUST LEARNED TO BE EVEN MORE GRATEFUL FOR THE THINGS THAT I HAVE AND TRY TO TAKE IN LITERALLY EVERY MOMENT WHILE IT'S HAPPENING. TAKE NOTHING FOR GRANTED.

Zendaya

I FEEL REALLY GRATEFUL TO BE IN A POSITION WHERE POTENTIALLY I CAN DO LITTLE THINGS OR WHATEVER I POSSIBLY CAN TO HELP ANYONE ANY WAY I CAN.

Elliot Page

IF WE ALL THREW
OUR PROBLEMS IN A PILE
AND SAW EVERYONE
ELSE'S, WE'D GRAB
OURS BACK.

Regina Brett

WE'RE ONLY HERE FOR SO LONG. BE HAPPY MAN – YOU COULD GET HIT BY A TRUCK TOMORROW.

Timothée Chalamet

SUCCESS IS GETTING WHAT YOU WANT; HAPPINESS IS WANTING WHAT YOU GET.

Ingrid Bergman

TWO MEN LOOK OUT THROUGH THE SAME BARS: ONE SEES THE MUD, AND ONE THE STARS.

Frederick Langbridge

**WE CAN'T ALL
DO EVERYTHING.**

Virgil

I'M THANKFUL THAT WE'RE IN A TIME OF DANGER – ABSOLUTELY – BUT WE ARE NOW WOKE.

Gloria Steinem

BEING THE RICHEST MAN IN THE CEMETERY DOESN'T MATTER TO ME ... GOING TO BED AT NIGHT SAYING WE'VE DONE SOMETHING WONDERFUL ... THAT'S WHAT MATTERS TO ME.

Steve Jobs

PEOPLE FROM A PLANET WITHOUT FLOWERS WOULD THINK WE MUST BE MAD WITH JOY THE WHOLE TIME TO HAVE SUCH THINGS ABOUT US.

Iris Murdoch

THERE IS PERHAPS NO BETTER
DEMONSTRATION OF THE FOLLY
OF HUMAN CONCEITS THAN THIS
DISTANT IMAGE OF OUR TINY
WORLD. TO ME, IT UNDERSCORES
OUR RESPONSIBILITY TO DEAL
MORE KINDLY WITH ONE ANOTHER,
AND TO PRESERVE AND CHERISH
THE PALE BLUE DOT, THE ONLY
HOME WE'VE EVER KNOWN.

Carl Sagan

WHEN I'M GETTING TOO MUCH
IN MY OWN HEAD, I TRY TO SAY
ALL THE THINGS I'M GRATEFUL
FOR. IT CAN BE SIMPLE THINGS,
LIKE IF I'M COMPLAINING
ABOUT HOW MY CELL PHONE
IS WORKING SLOWLY, I THINK
ABOUT HOW SLOWLY THEY
WORKED FIVE YEARS AGO.
IT'S OK TO HAVE GLASS-HALF-
EMPTY DAYS, BUT NOT TOO
MANY OF THEM.

Taylor Swift

GRATITUDE PROTECTS YOU FROM GREED AND ENVY. WHAT YOU HAVE IS ENOUGH. WHAT YOU ARE IS AMAZING.

A GRATEFUL PERSON IS ONE
WHO IS ABLE TO RECEIVE
GIFTS THAT OTHER PEOPLE
ARE PROVIDING FOR THEM
OR LIFE ITSELF AS A GIFT.

Robert A. Emmons

'TIS BETTER TO HAVE LOVED AND LOST ...

... THAN NEVER TO HAVE LOVED AT ALL.

Alfred Tennyson

**OUR WORK IS FOR TODAY,
YESTERDAY HAS GONE,
TOMORROW HAS NOT YET COME.
WE HAVE ONLY TODAY.**

Mother Teresa

HE IS A WISE MAN WHO DOES NOT GRIEVE FOR THE THINGS WHICH HE HAS NOT BUT REJOICES FOR THOSE WHICH HE HAS.

Epictetus

YOU NEVER KNOW WHAT IS ENOUGH UNLESS YOU KNOW WHAT IS MORE THAN ENOUGH.

William Blake

GRATITUDE HELPS US LEARN THE TRUE VALUE OF THINGS.

NO ONE CARES ABOUT
WHAT YOU'RE DOING.
IT'S ABOUT WHO I AM,
AND BEING OKAY WITH
WHERE I AM. I AM
GRATEFUL TO BE ALIVE.

Selena Gomez

I AM SO GRATEFUL
THAT I AM IN A SPACE
NOW WHERE I DO
GET TO CALL MY OWN
SHOTS AND I DO GET TO
BE WHO I WANT TO BE.

Jonathan Van Ness

I AM GRATEFUL FOR WHAT I HAVE.

**TO LIVE AT ALL
IS MIRACLE ENOUGH.**

Mervyn Peake

IN ALL THE YEARS THAT I'VE BEEN
DOING THIS SINCE I DISCOVERED
THE TALENT [WRITING] WHEN
I WAS 7 OR 8 YEARS OLD, I STILL
FEEL MUCH THE SAME AS I DID
IN THE EARLY DAYS, WHICH IS –
I'M GOING TO LEAVE THE ORDINARY
WORLD FOR MY OWN WORLD. AND
IT'S A WONDERFUL, EXHILARATING
EXPERIENCE. I'M VERY GRATEFUL
TO BE ABLE TO HAVE IT.

Stephen King

I LOOKED AROUND AND
THOUGHT ABOUT MY LIFE.
I FELT GRATEFUL. I NOTICED
EVERY DETAIL. THAT IS THE
KEY TO TIME TRAVEL. YOU
CAN ONLY MOVE IF YOU ARE
ACTUALLY IN THE MOMENT.
YOU HAVE TO BE WHERE YOU
ARE TO GET WHERE YOU
NEED TO GO.

Amy Poehler

I'M GRATEFUL
FOR ALL THE
TIMES THAT
I'VE LAUGHED
THIS YEAR.
THAT SOUNDS
CRAZY BUT AS
YOU GET OLDER,
YOU REALLY
TAKE A MOMENT
AND GO ...

... YOU KNOW WHAT, I LAUGHED THERE, I HAD A SWEET MOMENT THERE ... JUST ENJOY AND TAKE THOSE MOMENTS.

Rene Russo

O LORD THAT LENDS
ME LIFE, LEND ME
A HEART REPLETE WITH
THANKFULNESS!

William Shakespeare

HE HAS ACHIEVED SUCCESS WHO HAS LIVED WELL, LAUGHED OFTEN AND LOVED MUCH.

Bessie Anderson Stanley

I'M MOST
GRATEFUL
FOR BEING SO
IN LOVE WITH
WOMEN AND
GIRLS AND
KNOWING
THEIR POWER.

**THERE IS ALWAYS
SOMETHING TO
BE GRATEFUL FOR.**

THE BUTTERFL
COUNTS NOT
MONTHS BUT
MOMENTS
AND HAS TIME
ENOUGH.

Rabindranath Tagore

A PROPENSITY TO HOPE AND JOY IS REAL RICHES.

David Hume

A MAN TRAVELS THE WORLD IN SEARCH OF WHAT HE NEEDS AND RETURNS HOME TO FIND IT.

George Moore

I WANT TO THANK MY MOM, WHO'S GIVEN ME THE STRENGTH TO FIGHT EVERY SINGLE DAY TO BE WHO I WANT TO BE.

Halle Berry

I AM GRATEFUL FOR THE BLESSINGS OF WEALTH, BUT IT HASN'T CHANGED WHO I AM. MY FEET ARE STILL ON THE GROUND. I'M JUST WEARING BETTER SHOES.

GRATITUDE ERASES ALL NEGATIVITY BECAUSE THERE'S NO ROOM NOW FOR NEGATIVITY. IT'S NOT A MAGIC TRICK – JOY AND DEPRESSION CANNOT RESIDE IN THE SAME SPACE.

Steve Harvey

HUG YOUR OWN FAMILY TIGHTER TODAY AND BE GRATEFUL YOU CAN TELL THEM YOU LOVE THEM.

The Rock

**GRATITUDE
IS A GIFT
YOU GIVE
TO OTHERS.**

PERFECT
IS BORING.

Shonda Rhimes

THE DIFFERENCE BETWEEN SUCCESSFUL PEOPLE AND OTHERS IS HOW LONG THEY SPEND FEELING SORRY FOR THEMSELVES

Barbara Corcoran

IF YOU'RE GRATEFUL, YOU'RE
NOT FEARFUL, AND IF YOU'RE
NOT FEARFUL, YOU'RE NOT
VIOLENT. IF YOU'RE GRATEFUL,
YOU ACT OUT OF A SENSE OF
ENOUGH AND NOT OF A SENSE
OF SCARCITY, AND YOU ARE
WILLING TO SHARE. IF YOU ARE
GRATEFUL, YOU ARE ENJOYING
THE DIFFERENCES BETWEEN
AND YOU ARE RESPECTFUL
TO EVERYBODY.

David Steindl-Rast

[I AM] GRATEFUL FOR THE BLESSINGS OF HOME AND FAMILY AND, IN PARTICULAR, FOR 70 YEARS OF MARRIAGE. I DON'T KNOW THAT ANYONE HAD INVENTED THE TERM "PLATINUM" FOR A 70TH WEDDING ANNIVERSARY. WHEN I WAS BORN, YOU WEREN'T EXPECTED TO BE AROUND THAT LONG.

Queen Elizabeth II

GIVE THANKS FOR A LITTLE AND YOU WILL FIND A LOT.

OWN ALL OF YOUR MEMORIES AND EXPERIENCES, EVEN IF THEY WERE TRAUMATIC ... ALL OF WHO YOU ARE IS WHO YOU ARE.

Viola Davis

HAPPINESS LIVES IN THE MIND. THE MORE GRATEFUL YOU ARE, THE MORE YOU HAVE TO BE GRATEFUL FOR.

YOU SHOULD FEEL GRATEFUL
AND HAPPY THAT YOU'RE
HEALTHY, YOU'RE ALIVE
AND THAT YOU ARE LOVED.
WHATEVER WEIGHT YOU ARE,
WHATEVER SITUATION YOU'RE
IN, WHETHER YOU HAVE A
BREAKOUT, WHATEVER IT IS –
YOU ARE LOVED.

Ariana Grande

YOU CAN ALWAYS FIND ONE THING TO BE GRATEFUL FOR.

I WANT TO THANK ALL THE PEOPLE WHO GAVE ME THIS LIFE. I WANT TO THANK THE PEOPLE WHO GAVE ME JOY AND THE ONES WHO BROKE MY HEART. THE ONES WHO WERE TRUE AND THE ONES WHO LIED TO ME. I WANT TO THANK TRUE LOVE AND I WANT TO THANK THE WAY I LIED TO MYSELF – BECAUSE THAT'S HOW I KNEW THAT I HAD TO GROW. I WANT TO THANK DISAPPOINTMENT AND FAILURE FOR TEACHING ME TO BE STRONG AND MY CHILDREN FOR TEACHING ME TO LOVE.

WHEN I WALK INTO MY
APARTMENT AND I SEE ALL
THE THINGS THAT I HAVE AND
THE LIFE THAT I HAVE, THE
FRIENDS THAT I'VE MET AND
MY CASTMATES AND THE WAY
THAT I'M ABLE TO SHOW UP FOR
MY FAMILY – I'M AN INCREDIBLY
GRATEFUL MAN.

Antoni Porowski

REMEMBER TO HAVE AN ATTITUDE OF GRATITUDE.

FOR ME, EVERY
HOUR IS GRACE.
AND I FEEL
GRATITUDE IN
MY HEART EACH
TIME I CAN MEET
SOMEONE AND
LOOK AT HIS
OR HER SMILE.

Elie Wiesel

EVERYONE HAS SOMETHING TO BE GRATEFUL FOR. A FRIEND WHO REMEMBERS YOUR BIRTHDAY, YOUR HEALTH, A ROOF OVER YOUR HEAD.

**I AM ALMOST CONTENTED
JUST NOW, AND VERY THANKFUL.
GRATITUDE IS A DIVINE EMOTION:
IT FILLS THE HEART, BUT NOT
TO BURSTING; IT WARMS IT,
BUT NOT TO FEVER.**

**Charlotte Brontë
(in her book *Shirley*)**

NO MATTER WHERE YOU ARE IN YOUR LIFE, IF YOU CAN BE GRATEFUL FOR WHAT YOU HAVE, YOU WILL BEGIN TO SEE THAT YOU HAVE MORE.

Oprah Winfrey

I AM GRATEFUL
FOR THE WORRIES
AND PROBLEMS
I AM FREE FROM.

THANK YOU. THANK YOU FOR THIS DAY.
THANK YOU FOR THE LIGHT COMING
THROUGH THAT WINDOW.
THANK YOU THAT I'M BREATHING.
THANK YOU FOR EVERYTHING.
THANK YOU FOR THE PHONE CALL
THAT TOLD ME THAT I HAD THE JOB.
THANK YOU EVEN FOR THE PHONE CALL
THAT TOLD ME I'M NOT WANTED ANYMORE.
THANK YOU BECAUSE I KNOW YOU HAVE
SOMETHING BETTER FOR ME LINED UP.
THANK YOU.

Maya Angelou

WHEN SOMETHING DOES
NOT INSIST ON BEING
NOTICED, WHEN WE AREN'T
GRABBED BY THE COLLAR
OR STRUCK ON THE SKULL
BY A PRESENCE OR AN EVENT,
WE TAKE FOR GRANTED THE
VERY THINGS THAT MOST
DESERVE OUR GRATITUDE.

Cynthia Ozick

IF WE KEEP OUR FACES TO THE LIGHT, THE SHADOWS WILL FALL BEHIND US.

I'M SO THANKFUL FOR FRIENDSHIP. IT BEAUTIFIES LIFE SO MUCH.

**L.M. Montgomery
(in *Anne of Avonlea*)**

I WRITE, WITH A
PASSION THAT I FEEL.
AND WHAT I'M GRATEFUL
FOR, IS THAT I HAVE THE
SKILL, APPARENTLY.
SOMETIMES ANYWAY,
TO MAKE IT CONNECT,
TO HAVE IT CONNECT
WITH OTHER PEOPLE.

Alice Walker

LET US BE GRATEFUL
TO THE PEOPLE WHO
GIVE US HAPPINESS;
THEY ARE THE CHARMING
GARDENERS THANKS TO
WHOM OUR SOULS ARE
FILLED WITH FLOWERS.

Marcel Proust
(from *Pleasures and Days*)

**WHAT IS LOVE?
GRATITUDE.**

Rumi

INSTEAD OF TAKING THINGS FOR GRANTED, TAKE THEM WITH GRATITUDE.

NO DUTY IS
MORE URGENT
THAN THAT
OF RETURNING
THANKS.

GRATITUDE IS APPRECIATING WHAT YOU HAD IN THE PAST, WHAT YOU HAVE NOW AND WHAT YOU HAVE TO LOOK FORWARD TO.

LIFE IS A SHIPWRECK, BUT WE MUST NOT FORGET TO SING IN THE LIFEBOATS.

Peter Gay

ONE MUST FEEL GRATITUDE FOR WHAT HAS BEEN RATHER THAN DISTRESS FOR WHAT IS LOST.

Elizabeth Bowes-Lyon

TOO MUCH OF A GOOD THING CAN BE WONDERFUL.

Mae West

A JOYFUL AND PLEASANT THING IT IS TO BE THANKFUL.

The Bible

I KEPT PRACTISING GRATITUDE
EVEN WHEN IT SEEMED IMPOSSIBLE.
I CONTINUE TO THANK MY BRAIN
FOR THE AMAZING WORK IT DOES
AS I PREPARE FOR 12 MORE ROUNDS
OF CHEMO THIS YEAR. I WRITE DOWN
THREE THINGS I'M GRATEFUL FOR
AND WHY I'M GRATEFUL FOR THEM.
NO MATTER WHAT, EVERY MORNING
THAT I WAKE UP, I WRITE THANK YOU
NOTES TO MY HEROES IN HEALTHCARE.

Christina Costa

**OPTIMISM IS THE NEXT
STEP IN GRATITUDE, AS
WHILE GRATITUDE PROVIDES
REFLECTION ON THE PAST
AND PRESENT, OPTIMISM
PREDICTS MORE HAPPINESS
IN THE FUTURE.**

Sonja Lyubomirsky

SAY THANK YOU TO SOMEONE TODAY.

PRACTISING GRATITUDE STARTS WITH THE LITTLE THINGS.

I AM GRATEFUL FOR
MY MISTAKES BECAUSE
THEY WERE AN
OPPORTUNITY TO GROW.

A THANKFUL HEART IS NOT ONLY THE GREATEST VIRTUE, BUT THE PARENT OF ALL OTHER VIRTUES.

Marcus Tullius Cicero

GRATITUDE IS THE MEMORY OF THE HEART.

Jean Massieu

**BE THANKFUL
FOR SMALL
MERCIES.**

James Joyce

**JOY IS THE
SIMPLEST FORM
OF GRATITUDE.**

Karl Barth

DON'T DEFLECT COMPLIMENTS, JUST SAY "THANK YOU".

LIVE IN THE SUNSHINE,
SWIM IN THE SEA,
DRINK THE WILD
AIR'S SALUBRITY.

Ralph Waldo Emerson

**BE GRATEFUL
FOR YOURSELF.**

William Saroyan

WHAT AM I GRATEFUL FOR RIGHT NOW?

Published in 2023 by
Hardie Grant Books, an imprint
of Hardie Grant Publishing

Hardie Grant Books (London)
5th & 6th Floors
52–54 Southwark Street
London SE1 1UN

Hardie Grant Books (Melbourne)
Building 1, 658 Church Street
Richmond, Victoria 3121

hardiegrantbooks.com

British Library Cataloguing-in-
Publication Data. A catalogue
record for this book is available
from the British Library.

I AM GRATEFUL
by Hardie Grant Books

ISBN: 9781784886066

Publishing Director: Kajal Mistry
Acting Publishing Director:
Emma Hopkin
Commissioning Editor: Kate Burkett
Text curated by: Satu Fox
Editorial Assistant: Harriet Thornley
Design: Claire Warner Studio
Production Controller:
Sabeena Atchia

Colour Reproduction by p2d
Printed and bound in China by
Leo Paper Products Ltd.

MIX
Paper from
responsible sources
FSC™ C020056
www.fsc.org